The Lesson

by Judy Nayer
illustrated by Nancy Doniger

MODERN CURRICULUM PRESS
Pearson Learning Group

The Players

STORYTELLER	CHILDREN
PIÑATA MAKER	RICH MAN
WIFE	RICH MAN'S DAUGHTER

 ## Act One

STORYTELLER: Once there was a man who lived in a small village in Mexico. Every day he worked at home, making piñatas. The piñata maker was not rich, but he was happy.

PIÑATA MAKER: *(to his wife)* Good morning, dear! Isn't it a beautiful day? I can't wait to start work!

WIFE: Do you think we will earn enough money this week?

PIÑATA MAKER: Don't worry. I will take my piñatas to the market. We will make enough to get by.

STORYTELLER: The piñata maker had just started working when the doorbell rang.
PIÑATA MAKER: *(opening the door)* Hello, children! What can I do for you today?
CHILD 1: Can you show us how to make a piñata?

PIÑATA MAKER: Yes, of course!

STORYTELLER: The piñata maker loved to show children how to make piñatas. He whistled as he started.

STORYTELLER: The piñata maker put out the materials. He had already cut cardboard wings and a beak.

CHILD 1: Ooooh! May I put the wings on the duck?

PIÑATA MAKER: Yes, later. First I add water to flour to make paste. Next I paste newspaper all over a pot to make the body. Then I paste the wings and back onto the body.

STORYTELLER: The children watched the piñata take shape. Then they went outside to set it in the sun to dry. While they were outside, a rich man and his daughter walked by.

RICH MAN'S DAUGHTER: *(pointing)* Look, Papa! Look at what they're doing!

RICH MAN: Yes. They are learning how to make piñatas.

RICH MAN'S DAUGHTER: *(smiling)* Papa! May I watch too?

STORYTELLER: The rich man could not believe it. Although he had bought his daughter many things, he had never seen her so happy.

RICH MAN: Piñata maker! My daughter wants to learn how to make piñatas too. May she watch?

PIÑATA MAKER: Yes, of course! I like to make children happy. She can watch me start another piñata!

STORYTELLER: The next day, the doorbell rang again.

RICH MAN: Good morning, piñata maker! You made my daughter so happy! Her birthday is in one week. I want you to make the most beautiful piñata for her. And do not worry. I will pay you well.

PIÑATA MAKER: I would be happy to make a piñata for your daughter!

Act Two

STORYTELLER: The piñata maker worked hard all week. He designed the most beautiful piñata ever. It was a swan, as white as snow. It was so real, it looked as if it could spread its wings and fly. The piñata maker filled it with the most delicious sweets he could find. Then he went to the rich man's house.

PIÑATA MAKER: Here is the piñata, Señor.

RICH MAN: It is beautiful! Thank you!

RICH MAN'S DAUGHTER: Oh, Papa! The swan piñata is beautiful!

RICH MAN: Yes, it is wonderful!

STORYTELLER: Later, the piñata maker blindfolded the little girl and let her hit the swan with a stick until the sweets came pouring out like rain.

CHILDREN: Hooray! Hooray!

RICH MAN: *(handing him a bag of money)* Thank you, piñata maker. Here.

PIÑATA MAKER: *(looking inside the bag)* Why, this is too much money! It is enough for a hundred piñatas!

RICH MAN: Please take it. You deserve it. You made my daughter so happy!

PIÑATA MAKER: Thank you!

STORYTELLER: The piñata maker went home and showed his wife the money.
WIFE: We are rich! With so much money, you will not have to work. You will never have to make another piñata again.

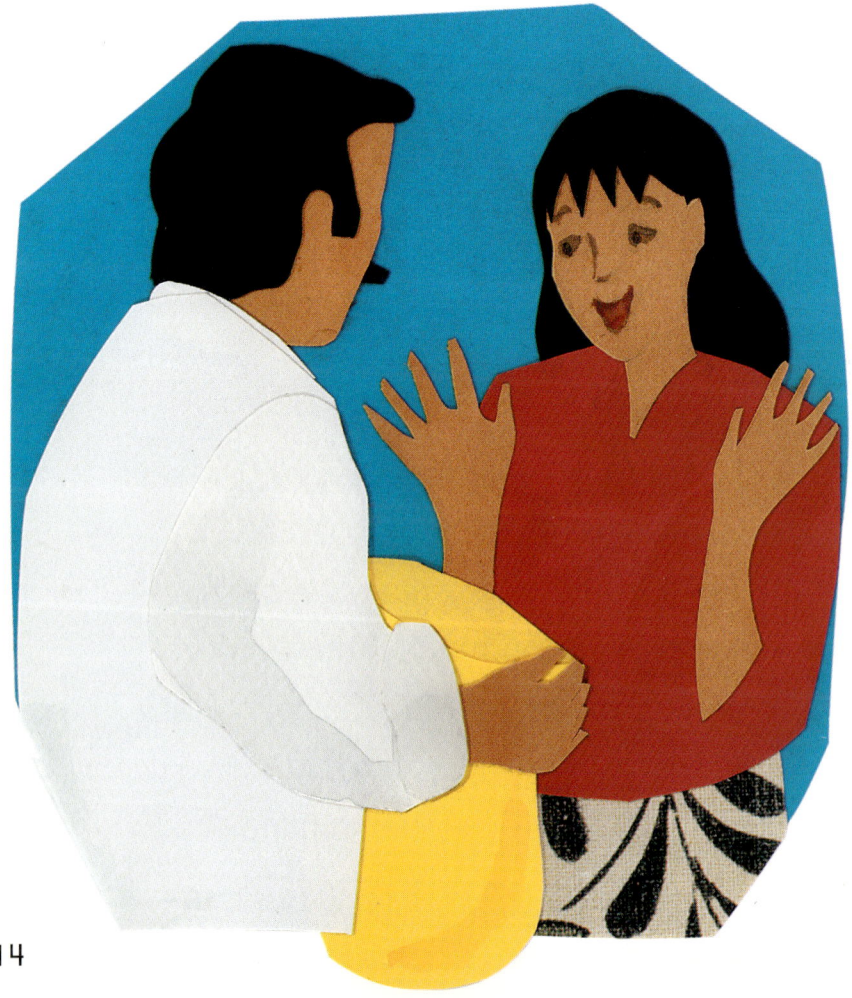

STORYTELLER: Days passed. The piñata maker liked having more money. But now he was bored and unhappy.

WIFE: What is the matter? I have never seen you so unhappy.

PIÑATA MAKER: I was happy when I designed piñatas. I miss creating them. Worst of all, I miss the children.

WIFE: Then you must make more piñatas!

STORYTELLER: The next day, the piñata maker started creating piñatas again. They were more wonderful than ever. So he sold more than ever. More and more children came to see him. Now the piñata maker was famous and very, very happy.